In The Hour Of My Heart

"A collection of poems that embrace the beauty of feeling everything and the magic of letting go, penned in the quiet hours of my heart.

Hermyne Khaling

BookLeaf Publishing

India | USA | UK

Made with ❤ on the BookLeaf Publishing Platform
www.bookleafpub.in
www.bookleafpub.com

Dedication

To the ones who feel too much, who love fiercely...

Preface

I don't have much to say about this collection—only that by reading it, you will have shared a moment of my life. A time when I felt deeply—about the people around me, about life itself. A time when I allowed myself to express freely, without restriction, on my own terms.
It isn't anything extraordinary, but it is real and true. This collection is a gateway to my freedom. May you find yours too.

Acknowledgements

Heartfelt thanks to my cousins—Glory, for being my second set of eyes on these poems, even from afar.

To Thangmoi, the most heartfelt reader—thank you for crying in front of me as you read my poems and for giving me the boost I so badly needed.

To my family—for understanding my long absences at home while I wrote this, and for letting me be lost in my own world without too many questions.

And to Kezevituo Zashiimo, who has been my greatest supporter from the very beginning—the one who motivated me, reminded me to write, and fanboyed over my words like they were about to change the course of history. Thank you for believing in me so relentlessly— even to the point of insisting I could take this entire era down. If I don't... well, you're entirely to blame for believing in me too much.

The Night Is a Poet's Hour

And so, I write poems—
of secrets, desires, wistful indulgences,
in the language of my heart,
in the hour of my heart.
I write them to the night,
and the night drinks them in,
without complain... like a true friend.

The candle leans in, patient and knowing,
melting slow, nodding to my silences.
It flickers when my thoughts grow restless,
as if it, too, knows what it's like
to burn without being seen.

The chair creaks beneath me,
It understands...
the weight of things unsaid.
It has learned my loneliness
in the way I sit too long,
watching shadows dance on mosaic walls,

palms heavy with things I cannot name.

The night endures my quiet confessions,
endures my muted outcries
spoken in the language of my heart—
a language only I and the night understand.
In the hour of my heart.

The night does not ask questions.
It does not demand explanations.
It only folds around me,
soft and familiar, whispering—
I know, I know.

I exhale into the hush,
and the night exhales back.
Here, at least, I am understood.

My Love is a Dried Flower

My love is a dried flower—
tucked between the pages of my Bible,
pressed where the psalms whisper.
My love lies still,
my love lies true,
like a summer long gone.

My love is a dried flower—
no wind has carried its scent.
Kept safe, unseen, untouched—
a love too delicate for daylight,
no lips have breathed its name.
It lingers, unclaimed in the waiting.

Maybe you'll find it one day,
when the paper thins and the years grow soft—
its petals still holding onto color.
Or will it stay here so,
folded between verses,
beautiful even in its forgetting?

Read Me Aloud

Read me loud and clear, baby.
Read me aloud on a July night,
as the rain taps on your window—
like echoes of a finger-picked guitar.
And tell me...
how do you find my sweet disaster?

A wildfire dressed in lullabies,
a storm humming songs in its sleep.
Read me aloud on an August calm,
Read me when the world is still.
Tame the wild edges of my history,
Chart the fault lines on my skin like faded star maps
don't just skim the sky, please.

Read me loud in December's chill
Read me raw and read me whole,
not just the verses I leave in the light.
Tear me apart and spill the silence,
poems buried beneath my bones.

The surface isn't the gospel, my Love—
Let the ink stain your hands.
Turn the page, baby,
Don't stop now!
and tell me if you still understand.

Love Don't Have to Last

Is it true that love don't have to last forever?
That it don't have to leave a mark?
That time will make it softer,
that the wind will smooth the edges—
old scars turning into stars?

Is it true that some love is meant to let go?
That some just pass right through,
like a note, a verse, a half-finished rhyme—
like something only meant to be dreamt from a distance,
like a shadow, like the moon.
Unreachable.

We fell in love on a midnight bus,
the world rushing by in a blur.
I can still recall that stolen night like a picture,
how we built our forever in borrowed time,
your shoulder brushing mine like an almost-promise.

You were the sunset, burning gold.

Your gaze stirred fire beneath my skin.
I swore the sky was ours to keep,
but you slipped just like the sea...
the waves...

Love Don't Have to Stay

Maybe love is meant to be fleeting,
like a match struck in the dark,
like a comet passing too fast to catch.

I closed my eyes just to make you stay.
I held my breath, watching you go.
I knew—damn, I knew—
that this love was made for goodbyes.
But I wasn't complaining.
I was so in love.

And now, I guess I should cry.
It's getting a little unbearable—
I hear it too often,
your name tucked inside a song.

Maybe love's not meant to stay,
not in this lifetime—only in rewind.
And someday, I'll have to make peace with it...
that quiet ache of letting go.

Maybe one day, I won't search for you
in the hush of a pilgrim's night.
Maybe someday, I'll believe
love doesn't have to stay to mean something...
Love don't have to stay.

A Love We Spoke of in Passing

We met like a flicker of stardust,
a spark of chance—
a strange chord strummed in the moonlit pause.
Voila!
Two clueless souls stumbling into something unnamed,
something unexpected.

And just like that—
you got me tangled in your mischief,
a little too in love,
a little too poetic for my own good.

Midnights stretch like old folk songs,
your voice humming in the quiet,
brewing daydreams between words,
laughing, teasing...

But we talk of futures we don't belong to,
of strangers we might learn to love,

of kids who will never know
the late-night echoes of our voices
cracking through the static of a call.
"Pardon? I didn't get that."
"Oh! Yeah, right. I like it too."

Then I ask, *"What will you remember about me?"*
And you say, like it's the simplest thing in the world—
"Everything to remember, nothing to forget."

One Day, We Will Be Strangers Again

One day, we will be strangers again.
Maybe not all at once, unlike a door slamming shut,
but like a tide pulling back—quiet, certain.
Slow, gradual, almost unnoticed,
until we wake up and realize
we haven't spoken in weeks...

Was it last September?
Or was it that December night...
You called and I missed it.
How long has it been?

Aphrodite wrote us on the same page.
Yes.
Painted our hearts with the same ink...
Yes.
But she could not follow through,
not with our story...
For shame!

One day, your voice will be softer in my mind,
like a song hummed from another room—
familiar, but no longer mine.
One day, my name will slip through your fingers
like sand on a sunset-beach,
blown by the wind to someone else's shore.

We do not belong to each other.
We belong to time, to change.
One day, we would love different people,
and they won't understand why
we speak in unfinished sentences,
why silence between us feels like poetry.

One day, we will be strangers again.
And it won't be tragic, just true.
So, we stand here a little longer,
we breathe it all in,
and then—
when it is time—
we let go,
like the sky releasing the last light of dusk.

Tell Me Gently

If your love wears off,
and if I should leave,
let me know, my love.
Tell me gently,
say it kindly,
and I will go.

I will leave not like the breaking of glass,
not like doors slammed shut against a storm.
You let me know —
tell me as if nudging me from sleep,
softly, slowly,
as if to wish me *good morning*.
Do not let it come to war, my Love.

Just let me know.

I will leave as the sun makes way for the moon.
Before the night takes over,
say it—gently.

And I will go like the last autumn leaf,
in time and in understanding.
I will go, cradling our love in my arms
Let it not be knocked over by anger.
Let it not be stained by bitterness.

If your love wears off,
and if I should leave,
let me know, my love.
Tell me gently,
say it kindly,
and I will go.

Love Came in The Midst of a Tropical Storm

Love came in the midst of a tropical storm,
just as the wind stole the roof off my house,
just as I stood there, soaked like a wet dog—
hair plastered to my face, grace abandoned
somewhere between the gutters and the mango tree.

I was in my overalls,
mud creeping up my ankles.
And then, there was Love.
Not standing in the doorway (because, well, no roof),
but right there, laughing under the gray sky,
as if my disaster was some kind of invitation.

Love could've called first.
Could've sent a letter in the mail.
Didn't give me time to fix my hair—
Didn't Love see?
I was a mess of rainwater and bad luck
when Love waltzed in, unannounced.

But Love came anyway.
Sat with me on my mother's porch,
smiled at my chipped nails,
my mud-stained knees,
as if I were some kind of masterpiece.

Then words were exchanged,
and I swear, I got tipsier
without a single drop of wine.
Love was kind.
Love was patient.
Love didn't ask me to be extraordinary.
Love only needed me to exist.

The Universe Says Yes

Often, in the comfort of my loneliness,
I close my eyes and wonder about you—
what it would be like to finally meet you,
to stand before you,
to look into your eyes
and feel the deepest stillness.

Somewhere, you are walking toward me,
through streets golden with lantern light.
You do not know me yet.
I do not know you yet.
But we're both searching,
both longing.

And when we meet—oh, when we meet—
it will not be a question,
not a maybe,
not a restless night spent searching for signs in the stars.

It will be a sure recognition,

a soft conviction,
like a dream finally remembered.

And the universe will say—
Yes.

Keepsakes

When we first met,
we could hardly pronounce each other's names
without hesitation.
But we kept repeating them anyway,
warm on our lips, anyway—
memorizing each other the only way we could,
like pressing a rose between pages.

And when we had to part,
wondering if we'd ever see each other again,
we held each other's names like keepsakes,
repeating them yet again—
like a prayer whispered in the wake of dusk,
not wanting to forget,
not wanting to be forgotten.

I bottled your name in a jar at home,
filled it with rose petals and fireflies.
And you linger...

You linger like a perfume,
made of words and memories.

All The Places We Loved

I took a bus ride with you through town.
The air smelled of rain and fresh bread.
And I was in love,
following you through seasons,
through rain-slicked streets and autumn kiosks.
I loved you like a child who feared losing his own
shadow.

At the old church, we stopped to light a candle.
Your face, solemn in the glow—
I think I left my breath in the silence,
whispering prayers for you among the pews.
I think I left my warmth on the park bench,
by the fountain where we tossed a coin together.
And you left your laughter on the swing—
I swear, it still sways when the wind comes through.
My heart, on the riverbank where we dreamed aloud.

I think the street artist stole a piece of my soul
because his canvas tells me

I belong to the colors beside you.
I think I left a wisp of my dream in the steam between
us,
in that little parlor where we sipped tea,
around the baker's corner.

And when we were through,
I found I had nothing left to carry home.
I had left pieces of me in all the places we loved,
and now, I am empty.

"*Take care of my dreams,*" I told you.
"*I left them somewhere between the tea and the music.*"
"*Hold onto my laughter,*" you said.
"*It belongs to you now.*"

And we stepped away,
never to be whole again—
not without the parts of us we gave to each other.

I Told a Gypsy About You

I told a gypsy about you.
Amidst a storm of sand and forgotten cities,
I told her how your name was the first thing I reached
for in the morning,
how your laughter echoed in the hollow of my soul,
how even the silence between us felt warm.

I spoke of your voice.
I spoke of your hands.
She listened, eyes tracing the embroidery of her skirt—
wine and indigo.
Then she sighed.
"Spare yourself," she said. *"Have mercy, child."*

She saw it—the way your name trembled on my lips,
how love had made a home in my bones,
how I carried you everywhere
without ever putting you down.
"Love should not be a fever," she warned. *"And you are*
burning."

But how do I explain?

That even if love is a wound, I would rather carry it?

That I would rather be consumed

than live untouched?

Somewhere Between Here and Someday

Somewhere between here and Someday,
we dream of a kinder world—
where love comes wrapped in certainty,
loud and sure.
But we know...
That love is sometimes quiet—
quiet, but true.

Love is a voice on the other end of the night,
a small, silly story before sleep.
Love is an imaginary street, walked barefoot.
Love is an old scooter that sputters and stalls,
breaking down at every turn—
and laughing anyway.

So we love in the way we can—
patient beneath the weight of the world,
subdued, but driven by reckless tender.
We make no promises we cannot keep.

We do not chase the future.
Instead, we meet each morning as it is,
pressing today into the palms of tomorrow.

Somewhere between here and Someday,
we love, as days go by.

Thieves of the Night

All we have is a night,
and it is not long enough.
Part of us - magic,
part of us - cursed,
but while we breathe,
we dine with the gods.

We drink their wine,
dance to lyres and harpsichords,
make love between heavens,
where time is soft.
When morning comes,
the world will end—
time will turn solid,
and silence will rule.

So now, we steal infinity,
pocket its shimmer,
and vanish into the wild—

Whatever may,
two little thieves of the night.

29

And Often, I Wonder About You

And often, I wonder about you—
like a wind chime in an unsettled breeze,
never loud enough, never quite gone.
Some loves dissolve slowly,
like footprints, like ghosts,
but some still burn—red as an afterthought.

Too sad to stay. Too sad to leave.
So I keep coming back,
like a child searching for its mother,
like a tide that knows no shore,
like a romantic revisiting the same old poem.

Time has taken us where time always does—
to separate evenings, to separate mornings.
Some love never quite lets go,
like autumn wind returning to trees
that have long since shed their leaves.

Though some loves are meant to let go,
some never quite learn how.
And often, I wonder about you.

My Father's Barn

My father's barn is empty still,
empty like a drawn out noon.
Once, I swore I'd fill it with grain,
golden like the stories he told me—
but the fields had other plans,
and the rain came late again this year.

My father's hands are cracked like the earth,
lined deep with seasons of waiting;
aged like the rock on the village mound.
I wanted to give him more,
more than this patch of land,
more than a life of calloused palms.

I wanted to fill his pitcher with wine overflowing,
But he only smiles and says,
"The land gives what it can."
And I only have my love to offer.
But my father's barn,
Oh! My father's barn is still empty.

Somewhere in the hills,
the river sings the same endless song,
the trees stand with the patience of gods.
And I—I stand here too,
learning to love what I have,
learning to let go of what I hoped.

Some dreams are meant to be just dreams,
not because they are too small,
but because the world is too big.
So I plant what I can,
love what I have.
listening to the hills hum my father's name,
my father's song...

But my father's barn,
Oh! My father's barn is empty still.

Mama, Let Us Be

The rain sings on the tin roof,
soft as a cradle song.
I press close to you like a newborn,
possessive and needy,
cheek against your shoulder—
smoke, turmeric, and the oil in your hair.
"Mama, I love you."

You speak of love in hushed tones,
of men who come like seasons,
of the way a woman's heart must learn
to fold itself into another's hearth,
to love like the river loves the land.

You say it's time for a bridal veil.
You tell me to pray,
for one who will carry my laughter
like a pocketful of seeds
and scatter them across his ancestor's fields.
But *"Mama, I love you."*

I want to pray for you.
For the rain to keep singing,
for your hands to never grow tired.
Let the world move as it always does,
*"But Mama, don't grow old.
Mama, don't grow far."*

"Mama, let us be."

Where a King is Made

My grandfather has no gold,
no silk to wrap me in.
His hands smell of firewood,
of rice husk and the warmth of a life spent
tending to things that ask for nothing.

But when I return to the hills,
the wild orchard is mine.
The trees, older than stories,
are mine to climb and claim.

Dust rises behind me
as I run up the old pathway,
dried leaves breaking under my sandals,
the air thick with the scent of wild peaches.

From the crest of the hill,
Grandfather sees me first.
He laughs—
"Ho! There comes my grandchild.

Now, all the trees in my orchard
are his to command!"

And so it is.
Wild pears crunch between my teeth—
no one stops me.
Raspberries stripped bare—
no one blames me.
Guavas, plucked and left half-eaten—
no one tells me enough.
they are mine to pluck,
mine to taste,
mine to be left forgotten on a rock.

My grandfather has no gold, no silver,
but I, belly full, heart fuller,
am made king
in my grandfather's orchard.

By The River, Falls Teshel's Hair

By the river, falls Teshel's hair.
By the river deep, Moshel weeps.
The waters did not return his love,
The water did not hear his plea.
So by the river, falls Teshel's hair.

By the river deep, Moshel mourns.
The reeds bow but do not speak.
The wind moves but does not tell.
By the river falls, Teshel's hair—
And the water has no answer.

"Could I even say I am yours?"
"Could I even tell you are mine?"
But the water has no answer.
For the broken, there is no balm.
So the river turns its guilty tide.

In the village, they said it was fair—

a debt for a life, a daughter for grain.
No silver was counted, no bargains struck,
only a girl led across the river.

By the river, falls Teshel's hair.
Indeed, falls Teshel's earrings.
Did she know he would come?
Did she leave a trail to follow,
for her beloved, to come and claim her?
To buy back her freedom?

By the river, a fiddle of sorrow,
strung with longing, tuned with loss.
And when the bow kisses the strings,
the river weeps, the trees bend low—
for love was lost, yet none took blame.

By the river, falls Teshel's hair.
By the river deep, Moshel weeps.

I Became a Folktale

I had hoped you'd return,
but love is no cradle—
it is a road that bends and parts,
and forgets its own way back.

I waited.
I thought love had a way of returning,
like migrating birds.
But days passed, and I became a folktale,
a story traded by the fireside.
"Once, there was a love like this..."
A tale no one is quite sure was real.

Was I ever real to you?
No one knows.
Did you love me?
No one remembers.
Did I live in your heart,
or only in my own telling of us?

Some still swear they saw you walking back to me,
that somewhere, in another life,
you did return.
But is it real?
No one knows.

I became a folktale.

February

A girl's heart is February—
wild with freedom, reckless with wonder.
Running barefoot between winter and spring,
never waiting, never still.

She is brown eyes, warm as worn-out pages,
a mind brimming with cardigan dreams,
lost in the silk of unwritten verses.
She's a song playing from a stranger's window,
a little too bold in her longings,
a little too lost in silly distractions.

She's a believer. She's a poet.
She loves easily, loves deeply—
like the rain that falls without asking,
drunk on love letters and cocoa steam,
never thinking of what comes next,
only *this* moment.

February.

She sees the world in dusted pink—
even in shadows and in silence,
the way poetry lingers in ordinary things.
A flower on the sidewalk.

A girl's heart is February—
wild, soft, untamed,
always in love... just as it is.
February.
And isn't that magic?